# ELVIS MEMORABILIA

# THE COLLECTOR'S CORNER

# ELVIS MEMORABILIA

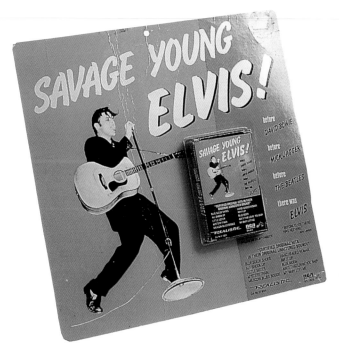

Grange
BOOKS

A Quantum Book

Published by Grange Books
an imprint of Grange Books Plc
The Grange
Kingsnorth Industrial Estate
Hoo, nr Rochester
Kent ME3 9ND

ISBN 1 84013-276-0

This book is produced by
Quantum Books Ltd
6 Blundell Street
London N7 9BH

Project Manager: Rebecca Kingsley
Art Director: Siân Keogh
Project Editor: Jo Wells
Designer: Martin Laurie
Editor: Madeline Weston

The material in this publication previously appeared in *Elvis!*

QUMCCEM
Set in Gill Sans
Reproduced in Singapore by Eray Scan Pte Ltd
Printed in Singapore by Star Standard Industries (Pte) Ltd

# CONTENTS

# BEGINNING A COLLECTION OF ELVIS MEMORABILIA

• • • •

*RIGHT Scrap Book, $400–500 (£250–310) in 1996.*

In 1956 the world of entertainment was about to be changed for ever by the emergence of a young man who was to become the most popular entertainer the world had ever known, so popular that he was soon widely known by just his first name.

Elvis Presley's impact went far beyond the music world and had a profound influence on American culture as well. When his first hit record 'Heartbreak Hotel'

reached the number 1 slot in the spring of 1956 it was the first time that a record had achieved top position in the charts of all three of the main music papers, *Popular Music*, *Rhythm & Blues* and *Country and Western*. In

*BELOW Record case, $450–600 (£280–375) in 1996.*

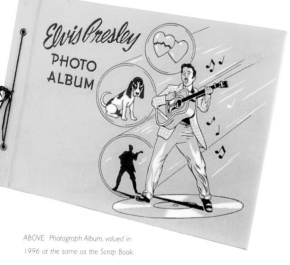

ABOVE Photograph Album, valued in 1996 at the same as the Scrap Book.

1956 alone Elvis had five number 1 singles, and so great was the popularity of his records that RCA was forced to use the manufacturing facilities of other record companies to meet the demand.

Not only the record industry flourished with Elvis's enormous success. The singer's fame was quickly transformed into the first 'celebrity bonanza' through the establishment of Elvis Presley Enterprises Incorporated.

BELOW Autograph book, value $450–550 (£280–340) in 1996.

What followed was an avalanche of Elvis merchandise with the appearance of Elvis's name and likeness on every imaginable item. Everything from items of clothing, costume jewellery and overnight cases, to board games, dolls, games and much, much more were available to his growing number of fans. This marketing venture was an immediate success and by the end of 1956 merchandise licensed by Elvis Presley Enterprises grossed between $20 and $25 million.

In the years since his first number 1, Elvis's popularity has remained undimmed, and an ever-growing number of collectors now seek scarce and potentially valuable icons of the past – the world of Elvis memorabilia.

## Elvis the Legend

To collect Elvis Presley memorabilia is to collect true Americana. The facts alone testify to the almost unbelievable popularity of the singer. Over 1 billion Elvis records have been sold (enough to circle the globe twice if laid side by side); he appeared in 33 movies, all of which were box-office successes; in 1973, via worldwide satellite links, a concert he gave in Hawaii reached a television audience estimated at 1 billion. Even more than 20 years since his death in 1977 hundreds of thousands of fans from all around the world travel each year to Memphis, Tennessee, to visit Graceland and to pay homage to the legend.

BELOW Elvis Diary worth $450–500 (£280–580) in 1996.

These five items all feature the same artwork and they are often referred to as the 'pink items': the record case, diary and autograph books are the rarest items. They all carry the Elvis Presley Enterprises 1956 mark.

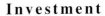

Much of the enjoyment derived from collecting Elvis memorabilia is due to the wide range of items that are available. As well as the items directly related to the music – the records and sheet music – there are novelty items, postcards, RCA memorabilia, pictures and film-related articles. Since 1977 a new range of merchandise has flooded onto the market, and collectors are adding some of these newer items, such as trading cards, decanters and dolls, to their collections.

*RIGHT AND BELOW The 1957 board game made for Elvis Presley Enterprises by Teen-Age Games Inc., West Springfield, Mass. It originally sold for $3.98*

## Graceland

As well as collecting the memorabilia, many fans find enormous pleasure in visiting Graceland, the second most often visited home in America. Since 1982, when it was first opened to the public, admirers from around the world have poured in. In recent years their numbers have risen from 40,000 a year to an estimated 700,000 in 1994. Graceland offers the visitor the opportunity to see Elvis's house and to pay tribute to the man, his music and his movies. Aircraft, including the *Lisa Marie*, which was owned and used by Elvis for both concert tours and general travel can be seen there, and there is a museum and small theatre. There are also gift shops carrying an array of the Elvis memorabilia which is being made today.

## Investment

As with all fields of collecting, many people look at Elvis collectables with a view to investment. It is true that many of the rarer articles, especially the novelty items that appeared in 1956 and 1957, have greatly increased in value over the last 15 years. A board game that retailed at $3.98 when it first appeared in 1957, for example, was sold in 1984 for $400

The value that can be placed on Elvis memorabilia is generally determined by the same criteria that govern the value of other collectables – condition, scarcity and demand. Other factors, such as detailing, craftsmanship and age, can also affect value.

*LEFT The dog tag necklace that bears the Elvis Presley Enterprises 1956 mark is more valuable when on the display packing.*

## Condition

The value of any given article will be affected by its condition: mint condition means it is clean and free from all damage and discoloration. An item that has been subject to considerable wear would be worth less than the same object in pristine condition.

Another important factor is the original packaging, which can add considerably to the value of any article. This is especially true when it comes to the jewellery that appeared in the 1950s. Most items of jewellery were sold on display cards. The cards themselves were often attractive and carried information about the maker and copyright. A piece of jewellery that is still attached to its original card will carry a considerable premium compared with a similar piece without the card.

Some kinds of merchandise were sold in attractive packaging, and the existence of the original box can really enhance the value of the article.

*BELOW These earrings had a 14 carat gold-plated finish and were made in 1956 to match a charm bracelet. On their original card, their value is increased considerably.*

(about £250). If that same game were to appear on the market today it would probably realize in excess of $1,000 (£625). However, no one should begin to collect memorabilia simply with the idea of making money. Acquire items that appeal to you – that you find attractive or pleasing because of their associations. Enjoy owning them for their own sake. If they gain in value over the years, that is a bonus.

**9**

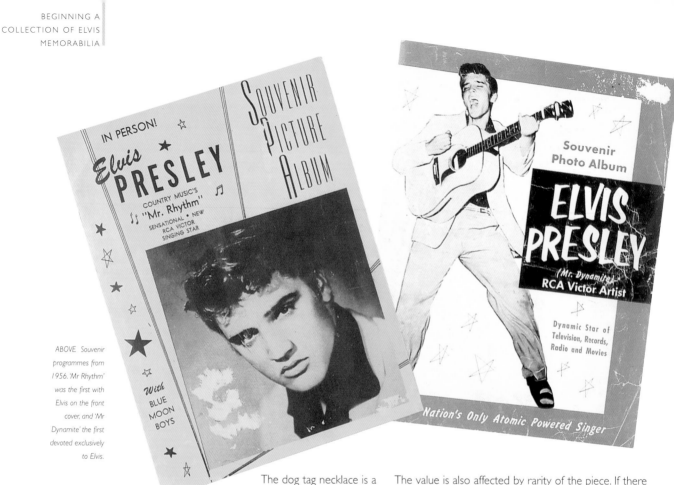

ABOVE Souvenir programmes from 1956. 'Mr Rhythm' was the first with Elvis on the front cover, and 'Mr Dynamite' the first devoted exclusively to Elvis.

The dog tag necklace is a prime example. It is not very rare by collectors' standards, but it is most unusual to find it complete with its original packaging, this adds immeasurably to the value.

A similar situation arises with the early 45 rpm records. Today the original covers are, in many cases, more keenly collected than the records themselves. In addition, the boxes in which the Elvis Presley leather shoes and sneakers were packaged are so rare that they, too, command a high premium.

The value is also affected by rarity of the piece. If there is a large number of an item available on the market its value will remain relatively steady. Nevertheless, scarcity alone will not add value to an article. For example, the 24-sheet billboard-size movie posters are very scarce. However, given their size and original purpose, the average collector has little interest in them as they are virtually impossible to display effectively. The one-sheet or three-sheet posters, on the other hand, increase in demand and value because collectors can enjoy them as decorative objects, and also because the quantity in good condition tends to decrease over time.

## Demand

The other factor that affects value is demand. Individual collectors who want a single item to complete a set will often pay more than a general collector. Dealers who specialize in this area may also seek to buy items so that they can attract customers or they may be asked to look out for particular articles. When the new trading cards were introduced, both dealers and fans were eager to buy the handsomely produced cards. Time alone will tell if they have the potential to become true Elvis collectables.

Sometimes rarity and demand coincide. A perfect example is the Paint by Number Set that appeared in 1957. This beautifully produced item originally sold for less than $2. In 1996, in good condition, its value at auc-

*LEFT The only doll made by Elvis Presley Enterprises during the singer's lifetime, and one of the rarest of Elvis collectables. The doll wears blue suede shoes.*

*BELOW A personal VIP invitation and menu for one of Elvis's Tahoe shows complete with outer envelope showing a photograph of Elvis.*

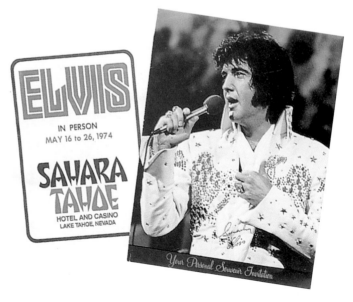

ELVIS
IN PERSON
MAY 16 to 26, 1974
SAHARA TAHOE
HOTEL AND CASINO
LAKE TAHOE, NEVADA

*Your Personal Souvenir Invitation*

tion would have been more than $1,000 (about £625) – it is one of the rarest but also most desirable of all Elvis collectables.

Newcomers to collecting Elvis memorabilia should remember that items dating from the 1950s and 1960s are well established as collectors' items. Few people who bought these articles when they first appeared had the foresight to know that thirty or forty years later they would be regarded as collectable objects. The guiding rule for any collector must be to acquire items that he or she likes. Have fun and enjoy the hunt, and do not let thoughts of future value prevent you from adding pieces to your collection.

This rule – that collecting Elvis memorabilia should be fun – is especially applicable to someone who is just beginning to build up a collection. Whether you pay a lot or very little for an item, buy something you want. This way, if it fails to gain in value or even falls in value, you will not be disappointed.

Items that were created during the 1950s or produced throughout Elvis's career merit being collected as such. When the first merchandise appeared, people bought the products because they liked them, and they used them for the purposes for which they were intended, often discarding them when they had outlived their use.

## Limited editions

A word of warning about merchandise that bears what might be termed 'intensified labelling' – that is, products which are marked 'limited edition' or 'collector's series'. In many instances, these labels mean very little and are nothing more than an easy means of enhancing the article to which they are attached and are only a gimmick to attract buyers.

ABOVE A scarf given to a fan at a concert in Louisiana, with a note written by Priscilla Presley.
RIGHT The Gold Sales Award commemorating the sales of over 500,000 copies of Moody Blue.

# CHAPTER ONE

# COLLECTING
# SHEET MUSIC

● ● ● ●

Collectors of sheet music have an almost endless number of subjects on which to focus – everything from historical issues to social life, politics and entertainment. Most collectors base their collections around a particular subject or topic, although collections can be built up on the basis of the composer, the kind or style of the music and the kind of artwork used on the cover, since the illustration used on the cover of each example of sheet music is vitally important to most collectors.

## Cover illustrations

Collectors of Elvis sheet music are especially well catered for, with over 400 song titles available. Although collections may be based on other criteria, many are especially interested in the vast number of photographs of Elvis that appeared on the sheet music over the years. This is a field of great interest to both the established collector and to the novice, for it is possible to build up a good collection without too great

*BELOW A selection of the many examples of sheet music available with Elvis's photograph on the cover.*

*RIGHT 'Elvis Presley for President' was performed by Lou Monte during the 1956 election campaign, included are two pins, one with the words 'Vote for Elvis'.*

*BELOW Further examples showing the range of cover illustrations used on Elvis sheet music. The same photograph can be found on different titles.*

expenditure. It is also one of the few areas of collecting where it is often possible to find better deals in second-hand shops or ordinary collectors' fairs than at ones that concentrate exclusively on Elvis.

## Different versions

Although there is such a diversity of choice, you will often find the same photograph was used on more than one song title from about the same date. This is especially, but not exclusively, the case with songs from the movies. For example, the covers of the sheet music of the songs from *G.I. Blues* are all very similar.

Sometimes the same photograph is used on the sheet music of songs from albums. For example, the songs 'Kiss Me Quick', 'Follow That Dream' and 'Just Tell Her Jim Said Hello' have similar cover illustrations. Collectors will also find the same song with different cover illustrations. 'Too Much' and 'Good Luck Charm' can both be found with different versions of cover photographs.

Among the most eagerly sought after sheet music is that relating to the songs from early in Elvis's recording career. Highly valued songs include 'Good Rockin' Tonight', 'Ready Teddy', the colourful 'Old Shep' and a rare 'Blue Hawaii' with a cover illustration resembling the movie advertisements.

Another interesting cover illustration is the cartoon likeness of Elvis used on the sheet music for 'Burning Love'. This cartoon effect is reminiscent of the style used for the Beatles' animated characters in the popular movie *Yellow Submarine*.

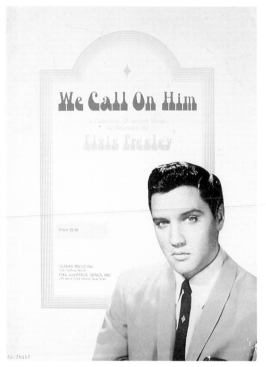

*LEFT A 32-page song book containing many of Elvis's popular gospel songs was published in 1968 under the title We Call on Him.*

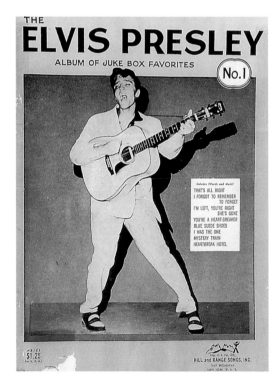

## Elvis for President

The rarest item of sheet music – as far as collectors of Elvis memorabilia are concerned – is not of a song recorded by Elvis, however, but a song about Elvis – 'Elvis Presley for President', which was performed by the singer Lou Monte. The song was produced in 1956, the year of a presidential election, and the sheet music was published by Vernon Music Corp. of New York City. At the time of publication, the sheet music sold for 50 cents. One of the few copies known to exist recently sold for $100 (about £60).

*LEFT The Elvis Presley Album of Juke Box Favorites contains many of the early songs recorded by Elvis, including 'Blue Suede Shoes'.*

## Specialising

Of special interest to some collectors are the pieces of sheet music of the songs that represent Elvis's poorest efforts as a recording artist. Most of these songs were recorded for the sound tracks of the movies in which he starred, and among the lesser known titles are 'Ito Eats', 'Yoga is as Yoga Does', 'Petunia, the Gardener's Daughter', 'Shake That Tambourine', 'Queenie Wahine's Papaya' and 'He's Your Uncle, Not Your Dad'. The sheet music for these songs is generally hard to find, largely because of the poor demand when the songs were originally issued. However, as with so much other Elvis-related material, interest in them has increased over the years, and they are now sought after. Whether you choose to concentrate on the sheet music of the songs from Elvis's early career or the songs from the movies, or whether you prefer to build your collection around the different styles of cover illustration, this is an interesting and rewarding area.

Remember that you must store and display sheet music carefully. The inks that were used on the cover illustrations often bleed, so interleave them with acid-free paper and store them flat, away from direct light and fluctuations in temperature.

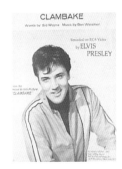

*ABOVE AND LEFT Five examples of sheet music showing photographs of Elvis at different stages of his career.*

# COLLECTING RECORDS

● ● ● ●

On a summer day in 1953, an 18-year old named Elvis Presley walked into Memphis Recording Service, paid $4 and recorded the songs 'My Happiness' and 'That's When Your Heartaches Begin'. According to legend, Elvis recorded them as a birthday present for his mother, Gladys.

## Sun Records

Shortly afterwards, Elvis received an invitation from Memphis Recording Service to return to the studio so that Sam Phillips, the producer of Sun Records, could lis-

LEFT The 1955 photograph of Elvis is sometimes referred to as the 'Tuxedo' picture. (right) The sought-after Elvis Sun promotional photograph displays an autograph.

ten more closely to what he thought was an innovative voice. Late in 1954 Elvis was playing a song – 'That's All Right, Mama' with which he was familiar. His accompanists, Scotty Moore the guitarist and Bill Black the bass player, joined in. The results of this session not only led to the issue of this title on the Sun Records label, the first of five songs recorded for that label, but also marked one of the landmark recording sessions of all time.

*THIS SPREAD shows the complete set of Sun Records 45s. Singles are highly sought after, and a complete set is extremely rare and therefore valuable. However, counterfeits do exist of both the 45s and the 78s.*

On 11 July 1955 Elvis recorded what was to be his fifth and last disc at Sun Studio in Memphis, Tennessee. The recordings of 'Mystery Train' and 'I Forgot to Remember to Forget' ended a magical era, and now Elvis's recordings for Sun are regarded as the very cream of his output. Not only do they represent the beginning of a remarkable music career, but for many they epitomize the hobby of collecting Elvis records.

Other records and items of merchandise may be valued more highly, but certainly from the historic point of view and their significance in Elvis's later career, these early recordings for Sun Records cannot be surpassed. But before you rush out to spend all your money, you should be aware of one or two problems with them.

## Counterfeit records

As with many other valuable objects, counterfeits of the Sun records exist. Remember that the original labels are a deep yellow with dark brown printing; most counterfeit versions have lighter or softer yellow labels with light brown or black printing. The original records were not made on coloured vinyl; they did not have 'Issued 1973' engraved in the vinyl and no original has 'RE' or 'Reissue' engraved in the vinyl. In addition, no picture sleeves were issued with the Sun originals. Authentic Sun records have either three indentations on the label, signifying a Memphis pressing, or a small triangle etched into the vinyl near the record label, signifying a California pressing. Purists may prefer the Memphis versions, the Suns that were printed in California may be rarer. Both are original pressings.

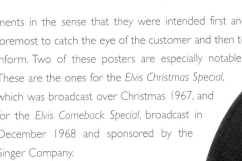

## RCA

The volume of advertising produced by RCA to promote Elvis's records is almost overwhelming. This chapter looks at the main area that the novice collector is likely to encounter.

### In-store advertising

RCA did a wonderful job of supplying record stores that carried Elvis's records and tapes with in-store advertising and promotional materials. This material included a wide variety of items, including posters, mobiles, rack dividers, postcards, catalogues, standees, photographs, calendars and record displays.

The posters that were distributed to advertise Elvis's latest 45 or LP release were, on the whole, very striking. They are similar to the movie-related advertise-

ments in the sense that they were intended first and foremost to catch the eye of the customer and then to inform. Two of these posters are especially notable. These are the ones for the *Elvis Christmas Special*, which was broadcast over Christmas 1967, and for the *Elvis Comeback Special*, broadcast in December 1968 and sponsored by the Singer Company.

### Postcards

Another effective way of advertising and promoting Elvis was the sale of specially designed postcards. These were especially directed towards the holiday seasons of Christmas and Easter, but they were also made for the Las Vegas concerts and other special events.

The Christmas postcards included a seasonal greeting from Elvis and Colonel Parker who was sometimes dressed as Santa Claus.

# RCA ADVERTISEMENTS

The record company RCA ploughed a great deal of money into promoting Elvis, and produced a dizzying array of advertising and marketing items. The selection shown here is the mere tip of the iceberg.

*BELOW Advertisement for the RCA Elvis Presley record player, featuring Elvis's gold inlaid signature on the top, October 1956.*

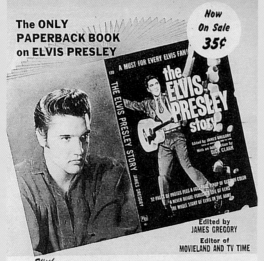

The ONLY PAPERBACK BOOK on ELVIS PRESLEY

Now On Sale 35¢

With an *Introduction* by DICK CLARK

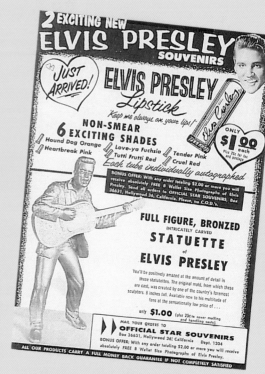

*ABOVE This advertisement was used to promote the first book published on Elvis Presley, featuring articles from Movieland and TV Time magazines and edited by James Gregory.*

*RIGHT AND ABOVE RIGHT Advertisements ran in fan magazines of 1956–57 promoting merchandise carrying the 1956 Elvis Presley Enterprises copyright.*

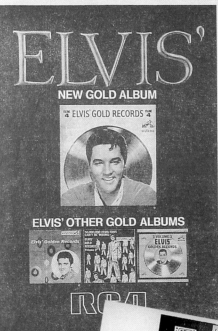

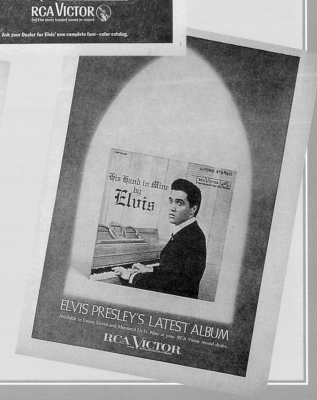

Christmas cards were produced for the years 1957, 1958, 1959, 1960, 1961, 1963, 1966, 1967, 1968, 1971, 1972, 1973, 1974 and 1975, those dating from the 1950s and 1960s being the most highly regarded by collectors with those from 1957 and 1958 holding the highest value. There are two versions of the 1959 card: one features a message from Western Union and the other is blank.

Easter cards were produced in 1966, 1967, 1968 and 1969. These showed a colourful close-up picture of Elvis, and on the whole they are relatively easy to find. Two versions of the 1967 and 1968 Easter card were produced. One version of the 1967 card has an advertisement for the album 'How Great Thou Art'; the other version is blank on the back. In the case of the 1968 card, one version has an advertisement for the movie *Stay Away Joe*, while the back of the other version is blank.

The 1969 Singer card was designed with the dual purpose of advertising the re-run in that year of the Elvis Comeback Special, originally broadcast on 3 December 1968, as well as advertising Elvis performing live at the International Hotel, Las Vegas. This card, and postcards from the period when Elvis was performing in Las Vegas or at Lake Tahoe, are both keenly sought after by collectors and therefore highly valued.

## Bonus photos

Many of the albums contained photographs of Elvis, which were inserted inside the album sleeve. These are usually referred to as bonus photos. It is thought that the first of these was a small card, 9.5 x 5.5cm (3¾ x 2¼in), with a picture of Elvis bearing the words 'Loyal Elvis Fan', which was inserted in some of the 'Touch of Gold' EPs. The same insert is said to have been included in some of the issues of the 'Elvis is Back' LP.

The bonus photos of the following album titles are the most popular and sought after among collectors of Elvis memorabilia: 'It Happened at the World's Fair', 'Girls! Girls! Girls!', 'Harum Scarum', 'Frankie and Johnny', 'Spinout', 'Double Trouble', 'Clambake', 'Speedway', 'From

Elvis in Memphis', 'From Memphis to Vegas/From Vegas to Memphis', 'Burning Love' and 'Separate Ways'. These bonus photos command a premium.

Four different black and white bonus prints, each measuring 25 × 20cm (10 × 8in), were produced to go with the albums 'From Memphis to Vegas/From Vegas to Memphis', and each double album contained two of the four different bonus photos.

An important bonus promotion by RCA was the large, 51 × 40cm (20 × 16in), colour print of the painting of the singer by June Kelly. This print was given away by record stores in the 1960s at about the time that the 'Roustabout' and 'Girl Happy' albums were released. The print has been reissued, but the modern version has a black border.

## Catalogues

Another popular subject for collectors are the catalogues of Elvis's records and tapes. The first listing of the singer's records was issued by RCA in the form of a picture card in 1956. On one side of the card

was a photograph of Elvis, while his recordings were listed on the other side. The first booklet-type catalogue was distributed in 1959, and several followed after this. Many were in full colour, and especially collectable are the record catalogues dating from the 1950s and 1960s. Special catalogues were produced for the 1967 *Elvis Christmas Special* and for the Singer-sponsored *Elvis Comeback Special*.

## Special promotions

In 1956 RCA had a special promotion in the form of two different models of record player, each bearing Elvis's signature. One model was designed to play 45 rpm records, but the other was a four-speed player. On both, the singer's signature

# PERFORMANCE POST CARDS

RCA distributed postcards to promote Elvis's live performances in Las Vegas and Lake Tahoe as well as to advertise his records and tapes. This selection shows cards produced in the 1970s.

*LEFT A card produced to give information about Elvis's appearances at the Sahara Tahoe on 4–20 May 1973.*

*ABOVE AND RIGHT A card with two close-ups was issued in 1970 for the shows running from 10 August to 7 September at the International Hotel in Las Vegas.*

*RIGHT A card featuring an advertisement by RCA for Elvis's 'Worldwide 50 Gold Award Hits' (volume 1).*

was stamped in gold on the top. The purchaser of the 45 rpm player received a copy of SPD-22, an extended play with eight songs on two records, and purchasers of the four-speed player received SPD-23, an extended play with 12 songs on three records. The four-speed model also had an instruction manual with a copy of Elvis's autograph on the front cover.

## Pocket calendars

Another promotion by RCA occurred in 1963 with the issuing of the first Elvis pocket calendar, a practice that was to continue for the next 18 years (the last one appeared in 1980). Each calendar featured a colour photograph of Elvis on the front, with the calendar itself and RCA's logo printed on the back. These calendars became especially popular among collectors after Elvis's death.

In 1980 RCA issued authentic reproductions of the entire set of 18 calendars. These were offered in a blue, open-ended container, featuring the RCA logo and bearing the legend: 'By popular demand – The 1963–1980 wallet calendars'. These reproductions were produced by Boxcar Enterprises, Inc. and bore a 1979 copyright. The reproductions are almost identical to the originals, especially the later originals dating from 1972 to 1980.

The most highly valued of the pocket calendars is the one produced for 1963, and this is easy to distinguish from the 1980 reproduction. The clarity and colour of the photograph, and the deep, rich red of the calendar, are quite distinctive. This particular calendar is also slightly smaller than the reproduction version.

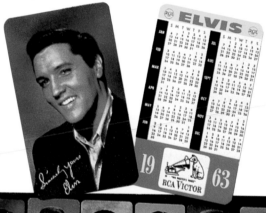

*LEFT The 1963 pocket calendar, the first and rarest of all the RCA calendars issued.*

*BELOW A complete set of original RCA pocket calendars.*

# CATALOGUES

A selection of the various catalogues distributed by RCA throughout the years that they handled Elvis's records. The purpose of the catalogues was to keep Elvis fans and retail outlets up to date with exactly what was available on record and tape. Catalogues were either issued on the reverse of photographs of Elvis, or in the form of more detailed booklets with a photograph of the singer on the cover.

COMPLETE LISTING OF **ELVIS'** RECORDINGS RCA® VICTOR RECORDS

ABOVE 1967 record catalogue.

ABOVE 1965 record catalogue.

ABOVE 1968 record and tape catalogue.

ABOVE 1969 record catalogue.

I hope you will like the new stereo 8 Sincerely Elvis Presley

**RCA STEREO 8** CARTRIDGE TAPES

TOP LEFT 1959 record catalogue.

LEFT 1966 catalogue for stereo cartridge tapes.

ABOVE AND RIGHT 1970, 1971, 1972, and 1973 catalogues.

# CHAPTER THREE

# COLLECTING ELVIS IN PRINT

• • • •

When the publishing world discovered Elvis Presley in 1956, it found a virtually inexhaustible source of interest to readers around the world. Elvis began to appear in print almost as soon as 'Heartbreak Hotel' reached the top of the charts in 1956. The fact that this was quickly followed by more chart toppers and that Colonel Parker launched the marketing blitz with Elvis merchandise kept his name in the public eye and fuelled an appetite for all things associated with the star.

This activity means that there is a wealth of magazines and fanzines available to today's collector of Elvis memorabilia, and although some

LEFT The 1962 annual Meet Elvis, published in softback, and the annual Elvis 1963 Special which was the first hardback.

RIGHT Hep Cats
magazine from
December 1954.

items are expensive, there is much that is affordable and this is a suitable area for the novice collector to begin to establish a collection.

## Magazines

BELOW 'The Elvis
Diary' from the
May 1957
issue of 16.

The story of Elvis in print began in the late 1950s. There were several teen magazines on the market at the time – 16, Hep Cats and Teen Life, for example – and there were magazines published by the music industry such as Rock and Roll, Best Songs and Songs and Stars. Later still came the mass-market magazines – such as Look, People and TV Guide which reached all age groups.

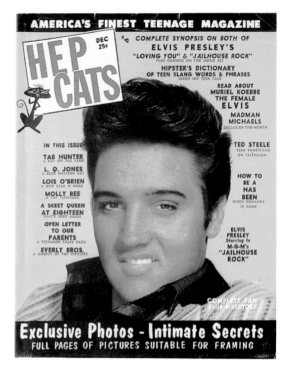

Since the beginning of Elvis's career, almost every magazine and newspaper in the world has, at one time or another, written about him. His picture has adorned the covers of at least one issue of every music magazine that has been published. There is, therefore, a mass of material for the interested collector.

The most desirable publications are those dating from the late 1950s. For example, the edition of Theater Pictorial that is devoted to Elvis's first film Love Me Tender, with an intensely brooding Elvis on the cover, carried an value of $250 (about £155) in 1996.

## Life stories

In 1957 Charlton Publications produced a comic book in its Young Lovers series entitled 'The Real Elvis Presley Complete Life Story'. The cover features a blonde woman holding a framed photograph of Elvis, wearing an open-necked shirt and hat. This comic book is now a very rare publication, originally selling for 10 cents but in 1996 valued at around $200 (about £125).

Also highly valued is an early publication entitled *Elvis Presley: Hero or Heel?* The cover carries a hint of what is to be found within, with the claim: 'Bonus insert: Life-size Portrait in Full Color'. In mint condition, a copy of the number 1 edition of the magazine can fetch between $135 and $150 (more than £85).

When Gib Publish Corp. produced *Elvis Presley in Hollywood* in 1956 it can have had no idea that a publication that originally sold for 15 cents would, some 40 years later, command a price of about $100 (£60).

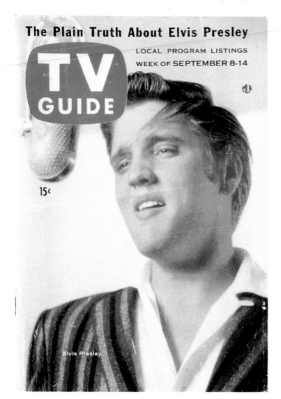

LEFT The first time that Elvis appeared on the cover of the TV Guide was for the issue dated 8–14 September 1956.

Not all of these early publications command such high prices. *Rock 'n' Roll Roundup* from January 1957, which has Elvis playing his guitar on the cover, has been valued at about $60 (£35), and *Record Whirl*, which had Elvis on the cover of the June 1956 edition with the question 'Elvis Presley: What's All the Shouting About?', recently sold for about $50 (£30).

By the 1970s Elvis had become something of a legend. He had already sold millions of records and made Elvis Presley Enterprises and Colonel Parker wealthy. He had made RCA records a force in the music world and was still selling out concerts wherever he played – which by this time was mostly Las Vegas.

## 1970s publications

In 1971 a special edition of *Screen Stars*, 'Elvis: 1971 Presley Album', featured articles with titles such as 'How Elvis went from singer to swinger' and 'His life story, his love story and his success story'. This originally sold for

ABOVE On the occasion of Elvis's return from the army TV Guide for 7–13 May 1960 featured a drawing of Elvis with Frank Sinatra. Elvis appeared as a guest of the Frank Sinatra Timex Special on 8 May 1960 – his first TV performance after his discharge from the army.

50 cents and in 1996 carried a value of approximately $30 (£19). *Circus Magazine Pinups* devoted its third edition to Elvis, entitling it 'The Elvis Years'.

Even at the end of the decade, Elvis was still getting plenty of coverage. In 1976 Ideal published *Elvis: The Hollywood Years.* May that year saw a *Tatler Special Issue*, 'Elvis: The Trials and Triumphs of the Legendary King of Rock 'n' Roll', which sold for $1 and is now worth about 20 times that.

In 1975, when Elvis turned 40, *People* magazine was there to mark the occasion. The edition for 13 January was on the news stands at 40 cents. Its value in 1996 was about $15–20 (£8–15).

## Newspaper features

National magazines were not the only publications to take note of Elvis. Both the *New York Herald Tribune* and the *Chicago Tribune* used pictures of Elvis on the covers of their weekly TV magazines, the *Herald Tribune* on 24 June 1956 and the *Chicago Tribune* on 7 July 1956. The *Washington Post* was more interested in the dying days of the Eisenhower administration, but on 19 June 1960 its Sunday magazine featured a youthful Elvis, tending to his hair, with an article entitled, 'Elvis Presley: He's fighting to stay on top'. In 1976 the singer made the

*ABOVE AND RIGHT The comic books Young Lovers from 1957 and Career Girl Romances 1966 aimed at the teenage market.*

*LEFT* Elvis
Presley: Hero or
Heel?, *a highly
prized publication
from 1957.*

Sunday magazines of two papers that were closer to home. On 19 August he was on the cover of the *Louisville Courier-Journal & Times* magazine. A week later his home town newspaper, the *Memphis Commercial-Appeal*, featured a concert photo on its cover.

But Elvis was good for sales across the nation. The *Houston Chronicle*, the *Houston Post*, the *New York News* and the *Long Island Sunday Press* were just a few of the Sunday supplements that featured Elvis at various times in his career. He proved so popular in Virginia that the *Roanoke Times Parade* featured Elvis at least three times in the late 1950s and early 1960s.

Elvis inspired publications devoted solely to himself. During his career the major and minor events of his life were featured in *Elvis Monthly*, *A Century of Elvis* and *The Elvis Pocket Handbook*. There was also *Elvis Today*, *The Elvis Encyclopedia* and *Presley Nation* among others.

## The local story

Getting your Presley collection under way or advancing an already established collection need not be difficult. You might begin by going to your local newspaper and asking if they have a copy of the edition for 17 August 1977 – the day Elvis died. That will firmly root your collection in your own locality.

# CHAPTER FOUR

# COLLECTING LIVE PERFORMANCE MEMORABILIA

• • • •

During the 1960s and 1970s performing at one of the major hotels at Las Vegas, Nevada, was regarded by many performers as the zenith of their careers. Therefore, when Elvis decided to return to the limelight with the 1968 Elvis Comeback Special, it was natural that an appearance in Las Vegas should be considered. Instead of the rigours of, say, a 12-city tour of New England, Presley and his entourage could make their base in a single hotel and perform in a series of lucrative concerts in just one venue.

The problem was to convince Elvis of this. Throughout his career he had always been conscious of, and remained loyal to, his roots. He also remembered occasions when he had not been well received. So when Colonel Parker suggested booking a series of shows in Las Vegas for 1969, Elvis might well have recalled April and May 1956.

On 23 April 1956 the singer had made his first appearance at Las Vegas. The venue was the New Frontier Hotel, and the audience consisted almost entirely of older, conservative people, who did not take well to the

young performer from Tennessee, with his new kind of music. When one audience responded particularly coldly to his performance, Elvis told them they were 'pitiful'. What had been booked as a four-week engagement was closed after just two weeks.

LEFT This special concert edition was a different size from the other tour programmes.

ABOVE This tour photo album contains 16 black and white photographs of Elvis.

RIGHT The Special
Photo Folio Concert
Edition (volume 5)
appeared in two
versions with
different coloured
covers, and three
pages differ inside.
They contain 16
pages of colour
photographs.

BELOW This
programme
appeared in three
versions, the top
was for concert
tours, while the
other two bear the
logos of the
International Hotel
and RCA. They
first appeared
about 1970.

RIGHT The Special Photo Folio Concert Edition (volume 5) appeared in two versions with different coloured covers, and three pages differ inside. They contain 16 pages of colour photographs.

BELOW This programme appeared in three versions, the top was for concert tours, while the other two bear the logos of the International Hotel and RCA. They first appeared about 1970.

Although this experience left him bitter, Elvis continued to tour the USA. He left Nevada on 6 May, and just seven days later he gave two shows in St. Paul, Minnesota. The next day, 14 May, he gave two more shows in La Crosse, Wisconsin, and on 15 May he was back in Memphis, where the police were needed in the Ellis Auditorium to keep the fans from rushing onto the stage. However he did not return to Las Vegas for 13 years.

International Hotel. This time he remembered the advice that Liberace had given him after his 1956 debacle: 'Dress to please the audience.' So, for his return to Las Vegas, Elvis abandoned the black leather that he had sported since the Christmas Comeback Special and instead wore a black, karate-style outfit for the opening night. However, he soon pioneered the rhinestone-studded jump-suit that became his trademark in the 1970s. He became the rhinestone cowboy.

## Return to Las Vegas

In July 1969 Colonel Parker was negotiating for Elvis's return to the desert turning everything in the city into a means of advertising the singer's arrival. On 5 July (after a brief diet) Elvis returned to Las Vegas and began rehearsing for his show at the Hilton

## The mature performer

On 31 July 1969 Elvis appeared at the International Hotel, and the audience were treated to a polished performance from a singer who was on top form. No longer the gangly teenager, Elvis proved he could successfully blend rock, rhythm and blues, country and gospel music into a balanced act. This performance began a series of 1,126 sell-out shows.

The first shows were in front of 2,000 people a night, with performances at 8.00 p.m. and midnight. By the end of the 29-day run, ticket receipts alone had brought in more than $1.5 million, and the International Hotel presented Elvis with a gold belt for holding 'the world championship attendance record'; the belt is now on display at Graceland.

## The souvenirs

Elvis's shows in Las Vegas created a whole new area for collectors. Dozens of souvenirs made exclusively for the Hilton International were available for sale in the hotel lobby, and the range included hound dogs, teddy bears, imitation straw hats, scarves, pennants, posters and lapel badges. Later, when Elvis started to appear at the Sahara Tahoe Hotel, the souvenirs for sale were similar to those sold at the Hilton International, but the Sahara's name was embossed on them.

From 1971, when Elvis began to give concert tours, merchandise specially created for the shows was sold in the lobbies of all the theatres in which he appeared. The wide range of merchandise included posters, photo albums, costume jewellery and pennants, and many of these pieces were also later offered for sale at the Las Vegas engagements. Many memora-

*LEFT Colour postcards of the Hilton Hotel, Las Vegas showing promotion for the Elvis live performances.*

bilia collectors prefer the associated items that were produced for promotional purposes, such as the paper and satin banners, complimentary shopping bags and posters.

Collectors also specialize in menus, and especially highly sought

after are the menus from the Las Vegas and Lake Tahoe engagements. From 1969 until 1976, a variety of menus were printed for the guests attending an Elvis show in these venues. Menus from the early years are especially desirable. None of them is more highly prized than the menu for Elvis's first engagement at the Las Vegas Hilton International in 1969.

Perhaps the most keenly sought after of the items produced for the shows at the Las Vegas Hilton International are the limited issue boxed sets produced in 1969 and early 1970. Both had the same cover as the commercially released album 'From Memphis to Vegas'. The 1969 set contained: the albums 'Elvis' and 'Elvis in Memphis'; a letter from Elvis and Colonel Parker; a 1969 records and tape catalogue; two black and white and one colour photograph (the colour one with an advertisment on on the back); and a 1969 pocket calendar. The most interesting items are the letter from Elvis and the Colonel and the box.

The 1970 souvenir boxed set was very similar to the previous year's, with the same cover, but with the date changed. The box contained: the double record set 'From Memphis to Vegas/From Vegas to Memphis'; a menu, including an introduction by Elvis and the Colonel; a souvenir photo album; a catalogue of 1970 records and tapes; the single 'Kentucky Rain'; a black and white photo (with information about the appearance at the International Hotel on the back); a press release; and a 1970 pocket calendar.

Although other souvenir packages were given to guests in later years, none of them compares in value with the 1969 and 1970 boxed sets.

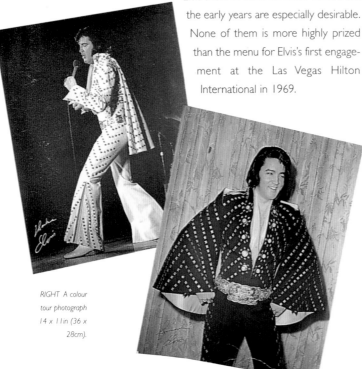

# COLLECTING CINEMA MEMORABILIA

• • • •

During his career Elvis appeared in 33 films, and the vast amount of cinema advertising that was distributed for promoting each title was not only abundant but artistically appealing as well. For each of Elvis's films, from *Love Me Tender* in 1956 to the documentary *Elvis on Tour* in 1972 there were movie posters, lobby cards, film stills, press books, standees and much for the cinemas to display to promote the films. All of these movie pieces are now regarded as collectable, and they are keenly sought after, although some of the very large items are less so.

## One-sheet posters

Among the most popular types of movie memorabilia are the one-sheet posters, sized (104 × 68.5cm) 41 × 27in – that is, the standard movie poster – and one-sheets were made for all 33 of Elvis's films. The value of the one-sheet poster can largely determine the value of other promotional material for the same film. One-sheet posters were printed on light paper stock and they were folded after printing so that they could be easily sent to cinemas all over the country.

Sometimes, when a film was re-released for a second run, a re-issue poster was made available to the cinemas. These re-issue posters sometimes varied from the originals. For example, the re-issue poster for *King Creole* had different graphics from the

*ABOVE A one-sheet poster for King Creole, considered by many to be the best film Elvis made.*

*LEFT A one-sheet for Change of Habit, Elvis's last dramatic film.*

original version. At least two Elvis films had more than one version of the original one-sheet poster – *Viva Las Vegas* and *Elvis on Tour*.

Posters that were larger than the one-sheets were also produced for advertising purposes. These are the three-sheet, six-sheet and 24-sheet size. Some of these are rare, but not necessarily popular with collectors.

BELOW An insert poster for Easy Come, Easy Go released in 1967.

BELOW An insert poster for Clambake. Inserts made an attractive display.

BELOW An insert poster for Flaming Star, released in December 1960.

## Larger posters

The three-sheet posters, which measure 206 × 104cm (81 × 41in), were printed on light paper and were supplied in two or three sections. They were produced for all 33 of Elvis's films. Depending on the popularity of the film concerned and the quality of the illustration, the three-sheet poster can command a higher price than the one-sheet for the same film. *Jailhouse Rock* and *Viva Las Vegas* are examples of this. On the other hand, if the quality of the artwork is good and the film is popular, the one-sheet can be more sought after, and therefore more expensive, than the three-sheet.

Six-sheet posters, which measure 206 × 206cm (81 × 81in), were printed on lightweight paper. Again, depending on the graphics and the popularity of the film they can command high prices. The size of the six-sheet and the space required to display it properly can discourage some collectors. The six-sheets for all the movies were sometimes not illustrated in the press books, but they could be ordered through *National Screen*. Six-sheet posters are very scarce.

The large 24-sheet posters, which measure 4.1 × 2.7m (162 × 108in), were printed on lightweight paper, and, according to the press books, they were made for all of Elvis's films except *Elvis on Tour*. They were intended for billboard advertising, and their size makes them unsuitable for most collectors. These posters are very rare because so many were destroyed, and very few survived unused.

## Window cards

Some of the most popular items of movie memorabilia are the window cards, insert posters and half-sheet posters. Window cards, which measure 56 × 36cm (22 × 14in), were printed on heavier paper than the posters and they

offer the collector a more reasonable outlay in terms of cost and framing. Most of the window cards, however, have writing along the top and many collectors prefer 'clean' cards, although the information about the venue and date does add to the nostalgia of the piece. Many of the window cards designed for Elvis's movies were bright and colourful, and at least two – those for *Loving You* and *Frankie and Johnny* – used a different illustration from the illustrations used on the other posters advertising those films.

## Insert posters

Insert posters, which were 91 × 36cm (36 × 14in), were printed on fairly heavy paper and many of these posters were extremely attractive, sometimes superior to the larger posters. The insert for *Love Me Tender*, Elvis's first film, with its photographic approach, compares very favourably with the illustration used on the one-sheet. These posters look very impressive when displayed on a wall, and their vertical size is a good contrast with the

other posters, especially the halfsheets. Although most insert posters were originally folded, it is possible to find examples that were rolled.

## Half-sheet posters

Half-sheet posters are also sometimes known as lobby photo cards or display posters. They measured 71 × 56cm (28 × 22in) and were printed on heavy paper. The half-sheet was available in two original styles for *Loving You*, *Jailhouse Rock* and *King Creole*, and an original re-issue with a different illustration was prepared for the re-release of *King Creole*. An R in the lower right hand corner indicates that the poster accompanied a re-release. The numbers following the letter represent the year the film was re-released, an identification number indicating the number of films the National Screen Service had printed during the course of that particular year. An original poster will not have the R.

*ABOVE LEFT*
*A half-sheet poster for the film* Tickle Me.

*ABOVE RIGHT*
*A half-sheet poster for* Viva Las Vegas *with Ann-Margret.*

# LOBBY CARDS

Eight lobby cards were produced for each movie, each showing a different key scene from the movie. They are considered some of the most collectable of all Elvis movie memorabilia.

ABOVE One of the lobby cards for G.I. Blues, released in October 1960.

ABOVE RIGHT Blue Hawaii, originally released in November 1961, was promoted with this lobby or scene card.

RIGHT One of the eight lobby cards produced for Wild in the Country, released in June 1961.

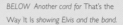
*BELOW Another card for That's the
Way It Is showing Elvis and the band.*

*ABOVE A lobby card for That's the
Way It Is showing a close up of Elvis.*

*BELOW Follow that Dream in March
1962 used this lobby card.*

*ABOVE One of the cards for Loving
You, Elvis's second film from 1957.*

## Lobby cards

Many collectors rank lobby cards among the most popular of all movie-related collectables. Eight lobby cards were produced for each movie. They all measure 36 × 28cm (14 × 11in) and were printed on card. Because they illustrate scenes from the movie, they are sometimes known as scene cards. The title, credits and release date of the film are printed along the base of the card.

Value usually depends on whether they show a close-up or a distant scene. Clarity and the significance of the scene are also important considerations. The dance scene from *Jailhouse Rock* is, for example, one of the most keenly collected, but cards that do not feature Elvis or any of the other major stars or that lack graphic appeal are often referred to as 'dead' cards. Sets of eight lobby cards for *Love Me Tender*, *Loving You*, *Jailhouse Rock* and *King Creole* were re-issued. The re-issued cards for *Love Me Tender* showed the same scenes as the original ones, although the sequence was changed. The re-issue sets for *Loving You* and *King Creole* are among the rarest

Some of the more stylish and colourful pieces of movie material are the posters that measure 102 × 76cm (40 × 30in) and 152 × 102cm (60 × 40in). These were printed on durable card stock and may have been made for all 33 films. Although the press books do not indicate that these posters were printed for some movies, the larger size has been seen for *Loving You*, *King Creole*, *It Happened at the World's Fair* and *Kissin' Cousins*.

There may have been more than one style of these posters. At least two of the larger size are known for *Wild in the Country*, and several different designs of the larger size are believed to have been produced for *Follow That Dream*. These posters, are among the most attractive of the movie-related items, but some collectors may be put off because of their size. The larger ones in particular are difficult to display well.

of all lobby cards. In common with other re-issue material, the re-issued cards bore the letter R, preceding the date the movie was released in the lower right-hand corner. Three of Elvis's films – *Love Me Tender, Jailhouse Rock* and *Flaming Star* – had title cards. These have a poster-like effect and are regarded as very desirable.

## Other movie memorabilia

Possibly the rarest of all the movie poster advertisements are the ones known as door panels. These measure 152 × 511cm (60 × 201in), and they were made for only a few of Elvis's films.

'Standees' are another rare and highly collectable item. These featured a posing Elvis on heavy-duty cardboard. They were usually between 1.5–1.8m (5–6ft) tall. Similar were the pieces known as 'hi-rise standees', which were used for many of the films. These were usually enlargements of the one-sheet poster, and they stood in the front or lobby of the cinema to promote the forthcoming film.

Still photographs, both black and white and colour, were issued for all but three Elvis movies – those three were *Love Me Tender, Jailhouse Rock* and *King Creole.* Both the black and white and the colour stills measure 25 × 20cm (10 × 8in). Many of the black and white photos and all of the colour stills feature the title and credits along the bottom of each picture. Unlike the lobby cards, no set number of stills was issued with each movie, although there were normally between 8 and 12 colour stills and

*LEFT A 'standee'
for* Love Me
Tender. *This is a
very rare movie-
related item and
highly collectable.*

**43**

# MOVIE STILLS

There were stills issued from most of Elvis's films, which were popular with his fans at the time and remain highly collectable today. Some collectors prefer them to lobby cards because of the good quality of the images.

*RIGHT A colour still from the film Live a Little, Love a Little which was released in October 1968.*

*BELOW RIGHT A colour still from the film Stay Away Joe which was released in March 1968.*

*BELOW A colour still from the film Girls! Girls! Girls! which was released in November 1962.*

"FUN IN ACAPULCO"
Starring ELVIS PRESLEY
URSULA ANDRESS · ELSA CARDENAS · PAUL LUKAS
Production · Technicolor® · A Paramount Release

63/264

LEFT A colour still from the film Fun in Acapulco which was released in November 1963.

RIGHT A black and white still from the film It Happened at the World's Fair which was released in April 1963.

LEFT A colour still from the film It Happened at the World's Fair.

THE TROUBLE WITH GIRLS
(And How To Get Into It)
An MGM Picture

69/182

ABOVE A black and white still from Flaming Star which was released in December 1960.

LEFT A colour still from the film The Trouble with Girls which was released in December 1969.

RIGHT A black and white still from It Happened at the World's Fair.

anything from 10 to 20 black and white stills. Because of the sharpness of the print and the attractive appearance of the colour stills, many memorabilia collectors prefer them to lobby cards.

*LEFT The press book for G.I. Blues.*

*BELOW The press book issued for the film Viva Las Vegas.*

## Press books

*BELOW The press book for the film Charro!*

Press books are very popular among collectors. A press book always appeared before the movie in order to alert the cinema's management to the material that would be available to promote the film. Press books also included a brief synopsis of the film, as well as outlining all the promotional material. The books varied in length and size. Those for *G.I. Blues, Loving You* and *Love Me Tender* are the largest. Press books are generally an excellent source of reference for information on the different kinds and sizes of poster that were produced for each film, although there are exceptions. The film *Jailhouse Rock* was unusual in having an advance press book as well as an original press book, and re-issue press books were produced for *King Creole* and *Flaming Star*. Intact press books command considerable premiums.

Small newspaper fliers, known as tabloid heralds, were usually purchased in bulk by cinema managers to announce the imminent showing of a movie. These fliers were often given away to patrons of the cinema, but they were also distributed to record stores.

Large, colourful banners made of durable, heavy-duty card were also used to promote the movies. These banners measure 61 × 208cm (24 × 82in), and they were hung in the front foyer of cinemas. The banners from

THIS IS MY PAID ADMISSION TICKET TO SEE

"G. I. BLUES" Starting Nov. ...d

MAJESTIC THEATRE

(Present at Box Office to Have Validated) Not Good Unless Signed ...

KEEP THIS

This slip must be present...
at Box Off...
valid...

AVAILABLE AT RCA VICTOR DEALERS

ELVIS' "G.I. Blues" Album

*LEFT The souvenir
hat for G.I. Blues
together with the
blue ticket which
served as an
admission ticket to
the film.*

the earliest movies are very hard to find. No one is certain how many of these banners were produced for each film. This author has seen at least one banner that was not listed in the press book.

One type of poster that seems to be overlooked by collectors is the double bill featuring the movies *Fun in Acapulco* and *Girls! Girls! Girls!* Posters of various sizes

were made available for this promotion, and there was also a press book. This is the only 'double bill' promotion known to exist, although the author has heard of a double bill for *Flaming Star* and *Wild in the Country*.

Other posters distributed by the National Screen Service are for the three films that were originally going to have different names – *Harum Scarum* (*Harum*

*BELOW A banner
produced for Stay
Away Joe.*

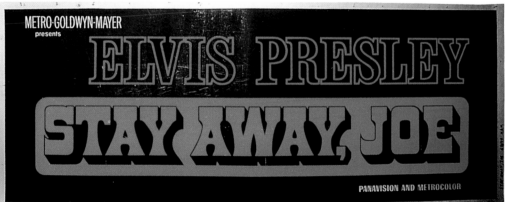

METRO-GOLDWYN-MAYER
presents

ELVIS PRESLEY

STAY AWAY, JOE

PANAVISION AND METROCOLOR

*RIGHT The
Hawaiian lei that
had the dual
purpose of
promoting the film
Blue Hawaii and
the soundtrack
album.*

identification numbers and reference information found on US posters. Most non-US posters do not even show the films' release dates.

The novice collector should be alert to the difference between re-issue posters and reproductions. A re-issue poster is an authentic movie poster made for the re-release of a film. A reproduction is an imitation or reproduction of an original poster. Reproductions are usually fairly easy to identify because their sizes are not identical with the original versions; they are also likely to be found in gift shops and they carry the manufacturer's name.

*Holiday*), *Spinout* (*California Holiday*) and *Viva Las Vegas* (*Love in Las Vegas*). Post and lobby cards with the original titles were prepared for these films, which were issued in Europe with their original titles.

Posters originating in countries other than America vary greatly in size from the US equivalents, and they also tend to be printed on much lighter paper. However, the colours are often much brighter and the graphics are generally better than the US versions. It is usually not possible to tell if these were for re-issues or for an original release, because most of them do not bear the

# CHAPTER SIX

# MARKETING ELVIS

● ● ● ●

Elvis Presley and his manager Colonel Tom Parker must be counted among the legendary show business partnerships. Unique musical talent was combined perfectly with a shrewd show business mind. Without the Colonel's promotional skills, the magnitude of Elvis's success could have been altogether different.

From 1954, Elvis was transformed from a singer who was well known in a limited area of America to a worldwide celebrity, one of the most idolized and influential figures in the history of popular music. Through music, television and film Elvis reshaped the popular concept of culture, and became the hero for hundreds of thousands of fans; part of this achievement was certainly the result of his collaboration with Colonel Tom Parker.

## Elvis Presley Enterprises

In the spring of 1956 Elvis Presley was incorporated and copyrighted in the form of Elvis Presley Enterprises, a move made with the encouragement and under the direction of Colonel Parker. 'Heartbreak Hotel' had just reached number 1 when Parker recruited a Californian promoter, Henry 'Hank' Saperstein, whose previous experience included the promotion of merchandise associated with the TV programmes *Wyatt Earp*, *The Lone Ranger*, *Lassie* and *Davy Crockett*. One of his great successes had been with sales of Davy Crockett's 'coon skin hat'. Parker wanted Hank Saperstein to market Elvis promotional merchandise. Under the direction of Parker and the guidance of

*LEFT A form letter from Colonel Tom Parker's office.*

Saperstein, Elvis Presley Enterprises contracted and issued a limited number of licences to manufacturers for items that would carry Elvis's name and likeness. The initial contracts scheduled more than 180 items for manufacture and promotion.

### Elvis as lifestyle

The first of the products to be mass-marketed was the charm bracelet, and RCA had exclusive rights to distribute it. More than 350,000 were sold in just one month, and this was followed by a veritable avalanche of merchandise — everything from clothes to games, jewellery to overnight cases. A teenager could be dressed from head to toe in Elvis merchandise and be doing homework with pens and pencils and notebooks bearing the singer's name and likeness, or playing the new Elvis game with friends.

*RIGHT AND BELOW These shoes, manufactured by Faith Shoe Co. were available in leather or in fabric; the box is very rare and as a result carries a high premium.*

When sales figures became available, one New York clothing manufacturer was shown to have sold 80,000 pairs of black twill jeans with green stitching, retailing at $12.98 a pair. Elvis lipstick passed the 45,000 mark at $1.00 each. Sales of the bronze statuette sold by mail order exceeded 150,000. It was reported that 240,000 T-shirts were sold together with 7,200 pairs of Elvis tennis shoes. So successful was this marketing venture that it is estimated that, by the end of 1956, Elvis Presley Enterprises grossed between $20 and $25 million.

After the boom year of 1956 Elvis Presley Enterprises slowed down its marketing efforts. Elvis's success meant that there was no need to promote the merchandise as vigorously. By the end of 1956 Elvis had made five number 1 singles and his first movie, *Love Me Tender*. He had become a major star.

## Continuing success

The following year, 1957, proved to be as dramatic as 1956. On 6 January Elvis made his third and final appearance on the *Ed Sullivan Show*. This was the notorious 'from the waist up' performance, because CBS censors would not allow the television cameras to show Elvis below the waist. Steven Allen, suggested to NBC executives that his own show, which was screened opposite the *Ed Sullivan Show*, be replaced by a movie. Allen had hosted Elvis just a few months before, and he was well aware of the singer's popularity. NBC did, in fact, show a movie.

After the success he had enjoyed in the music charts between June and December 1956, Elvis continued into 1957 in the same vein with four more number 1 hits. He also

appeared as Deke Rivers in Paramount's *Loving You* and as the rebellious ex-convict Vince Everett in MGM's *Jailhouse Rock*. Despite the critics who were scornful of his acting abilities, it was clear from box-office receipts that movie audiences were as enthralled with Elvis's presence as were the record buyers.

Although production was somewhat scaled down compared with 1956's output, Elvis Presley Enterprises were not totally quiet during 1957. Of the few new products that were licensed in that year, three of the items are among the rarest and most keenly collected of all Elvis memorabilia. These are the painting by numbers set,

*ABOVE A T-shirt promoting Elvis's singles and bearing the Elvis Presley Enterprises 1956 trade mark.*

*LEFT A grey felt skirt manufactured by Little Jean Togs Inc. Similar skirts in denim and corduroy were also available.*

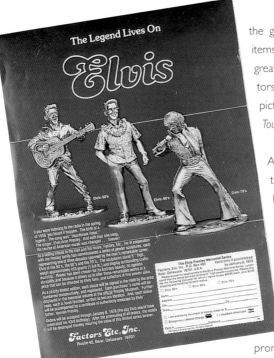

The Legend Lives On

If you were listening to the radio in the spring of 1956 you heard it happen. The birth of a legend. The song was "Heartbreak Hotel." The singer, Elvis Aron Presley. And with that one song, the course of American music was changed ... forever.

As a lasting tribute to the man and his music, Factors, Etc, Inc in cooperation with the Presley family has commissioned a series of pewter sculptures, each representing one of three decades spanned by the man's remarkable career. Elvis of the 50's, the 60's and the 70's. The sculptures stand 5" high, weigh approximately 453 grams (1 full lb.) and display outstanding craftsmanship. Pewter has been chosen for its lustrous beauty, its express durability and because it allows us to offer these remarkable works at a price that can be afforded by Elvis fans, and because of the power of the artist.

As a strictly limited edition, each statue will be signed in the mold by the artist, numbered consecutively, and registered. Each purchaser's name will be displayed in the memorial volume at the official Presley Museum. Further more, each is hand-finished, so that no two are identical. Each statue will be accompanied by a certificate of authenticity endorsed by Elvis' father, Vernon Presley.

Orders will be accepted through January 8, 1978 (the day Elvis would have celebrated his 43rd birthday). After the processing of all orders, the molds will be destroyed thereby insuring the value of this limited series forever.

**The Elvis Presley Memorial Series**
Factors, Etc. Inc. P.O. Box 484      Valid only if postmarked
Bear, Delaware 19701 U.S.A.               by January 8, 1978

Please enclose my reservations to the Elvis Presley Memorial Series. I understand that the series consists of three 5" high pewter sculptures. Please ship me the following statue(s) for which I agree to pay $49.95 each, plus $2.00 shipping and handling for each statue.

☐ Elvis 50's     ☐ Elvis 60's     ☐ Elvis 70's

Name_____
Address_____
City_____
State_____Zip_____

☐ I am enclosing my check or money order for $_____
☐ Charge my ( ) Master Charge   ( ) VISA/Bank Americard #_____

Card #_____
Signature_____

*Factors Etc, Inc.*
Route 40, Bear, Delaware 19701

ABOVE Even promotional items were themselves promoted. This advertisement is for a set of three pewter Elvis figurines (opposite page).

RIGHT Store counter display for Elvis bubble gum, produced by Factors Etc. for Boxcar Enterprises in 1981.

the game and the doll. Other items from this year that are in great demand among collectors are the 'glow in the dark picture' and the *Photo Folio Tour Book*.

After 1957, with one or two exceptions, Elvis Presley Enterprises actually produced very little. The exceptions were a gold-plated bust of Elvis, which was made in 1961, and a silver-plated necklace and bracelet, which was issued to promote the 1962 movie, *Follow That Dream*. In fact, although the gold-plated bust carried the Elvis Presley Enterprises copyright, it was actually a promotional item from the record company RCA Victor. After 1962 Elvis Presley Enterprises was not involved with the manufacturing of any new merchandise until 1982.

Before Elvis's death, merchandise bearing the copyright of Boxcar Enterprises was produced during the period the singer was performing on tour. The contract with Boxcar was drawn up in 1974, and it is reported that Colonel Parker received the greater part of the profits from the sale of merchandise, with Elvis himself earning 15 per cent of the total sales.

## Factors Etc.

Almost immediately after Elvis's death, Colonel Parker persuaded the singer's father, Vernon Presley, to join him in a marketing partnership known as Factors Etc. Incorporated. Factors Etc. was a company that had been founded by Harry Geisler in Bear, Delaware, and at one time it had global rights to Elvis merchandise and was the largest merchandising company in the world.

The contract with Parker and Vernon Presley related to all Elvis-related merchandise except the music and films. However, in July 1981 it was decided in court that Factors Inc. had no rights to merchandise the Presley name – so, re-enter Elvis Presley Enterprises.

## 16 August 1977

During the morning of 16 August 1977, just as most of the nation he had entertained and mesmerized was waking up, Elvis was getting ready to go to bed. Some time during that day, he died.

The reaction to the news was immediate and world-wide. Florists throughout Tennesse struggled to meet more than 3,100 requests for floral tributes to the King. Airlines throughout the USA quickly filled flights to Memphis as Elvis's fans began to make their sad journey to Graceland. President Jimmy Carter announced that 17 August 1977 would be a national holiday in the singer's honour.

In continuing testament to Elvis's title 'the King of Rock 'n' Roll' his popularity has continued almost unabated even as the twenty-fifth anniversary of his death approaches. Products bearing Elvis's name and image are still being produced and marketed, recordings are being reissued and sold as new albums, and movies, TV shows, documentaries, books, and magazine and newspaper articles continue to explore the story of Elvis's life and death.

## Movies and Books

Just a month after the singer's death Ronnie McDowell's song 'The King is Gone' climbed to number 13 in the *Billboard* chart. In 1979 McDowell provided the vocals for the TV movie *Elvis*, and two years later he performed in another TV movie, *Elvis and the Beauty Queen*.

McDowell also provided the vocals for the mini-series *Elvis and Me*, which was made in 1988. On 11 February 1979 Kurt Russell portrayed Elvis in the ABC-TV movie *Elvis*, a show that finished with a Nielson rating of

Other great musicians made their own tributes. Mick Fleetwood of the band Fleetwood Mac said that the news 'came over like a ton of bricks'. Bruce Springsteen said that word of Elvis's death 'was like somebody took a piece out of me'. Frank Sinatra told an audience in Wisconsin that he had lost a 'dear friend' and the music business a 'tremendous asset'.

The funeral brought the Mid South to a halt. Caroline Kennedy covered the story for *Rolling Stone*, and among those who attended were Sammy Davis Jr, Ann-Margret, James Brown and George Hamilton. More than 80,000 people queued to pass the open coffin and pay their respects, and a motorcade of fourteen white and cream-coloured Cadillacs, with motorcycle outriders, accompanied the hearse on its way to the Presley mausoleum at Forest Hill Cemetery in Memphis.

*ABOVE AND RIGHT The Love Me Tender body-care range and their carrying case.*

27.3, higher than both *Gone with the Wind* and *One Flew Over the Cuckoo's Nest*, which were shown at the same time. Also in 1979 Lena Canada's book, *To Elvis, With Love*, was published and in 1980 it was turned into a TV movie, *Touched by Love*.

On 1 March 1981 NBC-TV screened its own Elvis movie, *Elvis and the Beauty Queen*, featuring Don Johnson, who put on 18kg (40lb) to play Elvis, with Stephanie Zimbalist as Linda Thompson.

## Graceland

By the early 1980s Graceland was almost equal in public importance as the White House. Fans flocked there for anniversaries and memorials. On 7 June 1981 Priscilla Presley opened the mansion to the public, although the upper storey, with Elvis's bedroom and private chambers, has never been on public view. The house is now the second most visited house in the US. By 1991 it was estimated that the house earned more than $50 million annually and receipts were as much as $20,000 a day from tour tickets alone.

In 1981 the potential of Elvis's posthumous earnings became clear. Todd Slaughter, a member of Elvis's UK fan club, released the album 'Inspirations', which contained previously released gospel songs and which got to number 5 in the charts. This was followed in October 1982 when RCA released 'The Elvis Medley', which included 'Suspicious Minds', 'Teddy Bear', 'Burning Love', 'Jailhouse Rock', 'Don't Be Cruel' and 'Hound Dog'.

LEFT *The popular Sgt Elvis mini decanter, produced in 1984 by Elvis Presley Enterprises.*

## Recent memorabilia

By 1978 the modern Elvis memorabilia industry had begun to get into gear, and in October of that year *People* magazine noted that a 'billion dollar industry' had been spawned when Elvis died, ranging from $1.00 bills (Elvis replaced George Washington) to toilet seats. In August 1984 *Life* magazine was able to comment that

Elvis was not only worth more dead than alive but that his memory was 'earning 10 times what he made in his 42 years – and that was $100 million'.

In the years immediately after Elvis's death merchandising was uncoordinated and many poorly made products appeared on the scene, to be quickly discounted by fans and collectors alike. It was not until 1982 that Elvis Presley Enterprises Inc. gained control over the rights to the singer's name and merchandise, and since then it has been actively exercising that control.

More than 100 companies, large and small, all over the world were granted licences by Elvis Presley Enterprises to produce merchandise, and there have been some lines that have delighted both fans and collectors. Under EPE's control, the creativity and quality of much of the merchandise has been outstanding, and the good quality memorabilia being produced is a rewarding area for the collector.

The range of memorabilia has become so wide it even includes such products as Natural Choice Industries' 'Love Me Tender' conditioning shampoo, hair rinse, bath milk and lotion. These Elvis theme toiletries were marketed in what is now considered to be a very rare carrying case.

*RIGHT AND BELOW A brass plated Christmas tree ornament, produced by the Hallmark Company under license from Elvis Presley Enterprises.*

## Plates

In a more traditional vein, several companies have produced Elvis plates. Royal Orleans of New Orleans, Louisiana, produced a series of commemoratives depicting Elvis at some of his better known concerts, including 'Live in Las Vegas', 'Aloha from Hawaii' and the 'Mississippi Benefit Concert'. The plates originally retailed for approximately $35.

Bill Jacobsen designed a commemorative plate rimmed with 24 carat gold and featuring four versions of Elvis.

The plate, manufactured by Nostalgia Collectibles, originally retailed for approximately $45. In 1977 Limoges of France was commissioned to create an official commemorative plate featuring a portrait of the young Elvis. The 19.5cm (7 ½in) version sold for $25, and the 25cm (10in) plate was priced at $50.

In 1988 the first Delphi collector plate series to feature Elvis was offered through the Bradford Exchange. Eight different series, consisting of as many as 16 different plates in a single series, have since been created. They have become popular among collectors, and the value of the first such plate, 'Elvis at the Gates of Graceland' has increased substantially since its appearance in 1988.

Other plates held in high regard among collectors are those created by the artist Susie Morton and distributed by R.J. Ernst Enterprises Inc. The plate entitled 'A Commemorative to Elvis' is especially collectable.

## Dolls

Collectable dolls have ranged from the shoddy and gaudy to good quality items that represent the true spirit of Elvis. Soon after his death, a radio in the shape of a doll appeared in Hong Kong. This was exactly the kind of product that Elvis Presley Enterprises Inc. tried to stop. To combat this, World Doll was licensed to produce the Elvis Presley Limited Doll Series. The five dolls were sculpted by Joyce Christopher. Four of them stand 54cm (21in) high and sold for $100–125. One of the dolls, a 48cm (19in) 'gold and platinum' doll, sold for $285.

*LEFT A commemorative plate designed by Bill Jacobson. It was part of a limited edition celebrating the 50th anniversary of Elvis's birth.*

# MODERN MERCHANDISING

The marketing of Elvis continues even over twenty years after his death. He remains one of the most readily recognized icons of the modern world with new fans beginning to collect memorabilia all the time.

*RIGHT A modern game produced by Elvis Presley Enterprises in 1987.*

*BELOW RCA Special Products released and marketed the cassette tape 'Savage Young Elvis', which was never produced on vinyl, in 1984.*

The game that allows the legend to live on!

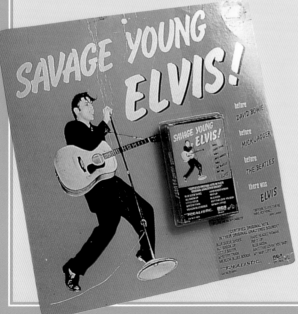

*ABOVE AND RIGHT In 1985 Nostalgia Collecctibles produced a set of four mugs, trimmed with 24 carat gold, to celebrate the 50th anniversary of Elvis's birth.*

*RIGHT AND ABOVE  Nostalgia Collectibles also produced a series of plates to match its celebration mugs.*

In 1984 the Eugene Doll & Novelty Company produced a series of Elvis dolls, and today both these and
the World Doll product are sought after by collectors.

One range of merchandise that was handsomely
crafted and beautifully packaged was the series of dolls
by Hasboro, marketed under the title 'Elvis Presley
Commemorative Collection'. These were manufactured
in 1993 and depict various stages of the singer's career.
Although six dolls are known to have been made, only
three have, thus far, been marketed.

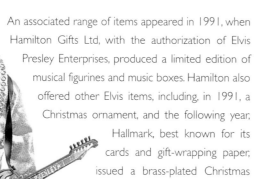

An associated range of items appeared in 1991, when
Hamilton Gifts Ltd, with the authorization of Elvis
Presley Enterprises, produced a limited edition of
musical figurines and music boxes. Hamilton also
offered other Elvis items, including, in 1991, a
Christmas ornament, and the following year,
Hallmark, best known for its
cards and gift-wrapping paper,
issued a brass-plated Christmas
ornament, retailing at $14.75.

## Cards

In 1956 EPE had authorized Topps Gum Co. to issue
a set of 66 Elvis bubble gum cards, and the value of
these cards has increased considerably.

In 1978 the licence for the cards went to the
Donruss Co. of Memphis, and they produced
cards that sold for 15 cents a pack. In 1956

each card was hand coloured,
but the Donruss set uses colour only if the original photograph was in colour. The value of the Donruss cards
has risen comparatively slowly.

In 1992 the River Group Company was authorized by
Elvis Presley Enterprises to print three series of cards
depicting the singer's life and career. The complete set,
entitled 'The Elvis Collection' featured 660 cards in both
colour and black and white, and it included some spec-
tacular photographs. The set also included a limited
number (40 in each series) of 'foiled' cards, known as
'chase' cards, which carry a high premium among collectors. The whole set is extremely attractive and is certain to rise in value.

In addition to the series of cards in 'The Elvis Collection', the River Group Company produced related items. Customers could, for example, obtain a binder with plastic sleeves in which to store and display their cards, and it was also possible to obtain a large, colourful poster promoting 'The Elvis Collection'. The same company also produced two other sets – one, of 50 cards, features Elvis's gold and platinum records, while the other, containing 25 cards, is entitled 'Quotable Elvis'. There was also a set of 25 colour postcards, each 18 × 12.5cm (7 × 5in).

Items related to 'The Elvis Collection' but not available by order from the River Group Company are the highly collectable life-size standees, which were made specifically for stores to promote the various series. The company also sent out promotional cards to retailers, to introduce and explain the series of cards. Only 10 versions of these 'promo' cards were made, and each bears the word 'PROMO' in bold type on the back. The most keenly collected of these promotional cards are those in uncut strips of four.

## Clocks and Watches

Perhaps because Elvis had a timeless talent, Bradley Time produces a range of clocks and watches, which include a wrist watch, pocket watch, two wall clocks and a travel alarm.

The Pearl Grandfather Clock Co. produced a limited edition of the Graceland grandfather clock in 1985. Each of the 6,000 clocks is hand carved from oak and features bevelled glass and brass fittings.

## Miscellaneous

In 1984 the Lapin Products Company produced two toy guitars, each copyright Elvis Presley Enterprises 1984. The large black and white, six-string guitar, trimmed with gold featured two decals of Elvis from the 1970s on the face. The smaller, four-string version was similar, except the decal on the face was of Elvis from the 1950s. In addition the background of the packaging of the four-string guitar features three tinted photographs of Elvis from the 1950s.

*THIS PAGE Clocks and watches were some of the better quality Elvis merchandise produced. These were created by Bradley Time Division, Elgin National Industries, Inc. for Elvis Presley Enterprises in 1984.*

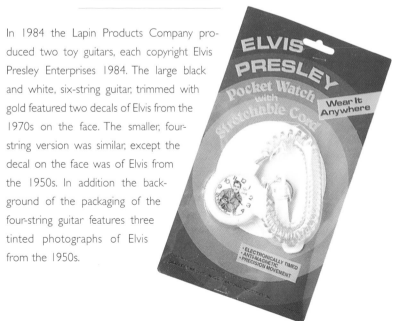

At the other end of the scale, in 1979 Boxcar Enterprises ordered 100,000 cases of 'Always Elvis' Blanc d'Oro wine, from the Frontenac Vineyards of Italy and sold for $4 a bottle.

The McCormick Distilling Company produced a series of decanters, the first of which, 'Elvis '77', appeared in 1977. This was quickly followed by 'Elvis '55' and 'Elvis '68'. All the decanters were authorized by Boxcar Enterprises, which also licensed another keenly collected decanter, 'Aloha Elvis'. Since then, there have been other decanters, including a series that featured Elvis with various pet animals Other popular decanters were 'Karate Elvis' and 'Sgt. Elvis'. McCormick produced smaller versions of its most popular decanters, which they marketed as 'mini-decanters'.

The McCormick Distilling Company also produced a range of white designer decanters, which consists of three different figurines. These may well be the most valuable and attractive of all the decanters.

CUI Inc. has issued several different styles of beer steins, including 'The Elvis Postal Stein', which commemorates the famous Elvis postage stamp.

*ABOVE A porcelain figurine of Elvis contains a cassette player which plays five of Elvis's hits.*

*RIGHT A porcelain figurine of Elvis in the 1950s. It was made by Avon Products in 1987*

## Postage stamps

It took years of lobbying the US Postal Service (USPS), but Elvis's fans eventually persuaded the USPS to produce an Elvis Presley stamp, and in January 1992 it announced that the singer would be featured on a stamp released on what would have been his 58th birthday, 8 January 1993. The USPS allowed Americans to vote on which image they wanted to see on the stamp – choosing between a 1950s Elvis as a slim, dark-haired boy, leaning forwards and singing into a microphone or a heavier, older Elvis, from the 1970s, wearing a rhinestone-studded jump-suit and singing.

A set of promotional material accompanied the stamp. Different packages of the stamp could be bought for between $5 and $20, and the entire pack of memorabilia could be purchased for $44. Millions of fans called in and placed their orders. The stamp depicting the younger Elvis proved to be the most popular.

Eventually the USPS ordered 1 million stamps, a figure almost double all other first printing and unprecedented in US postal history. By the end of 1993 it had become the most profitable stamp in the history of the US Postal Service. The average stamp issued will bring in approximately $2 million, while a stamp featuring a celebrity can bring in $5 million. In its first year, the Elvis stamp sold between $32 million and $36 million.

RIGHT The original 1992 US Post Office poster (far right) asked the American public to help to choose the image for the Elvis Presley stamp. Specially made voting cards were issued (right) showing the two designs.

In all the hyperbole and anxiety surrounding the issue of the stamp, some confusion was inevitable, creating a collectable for both Elvis fans and philatelists. The postal service mistakenly shipped thousands of the stamps to Amarillo, Texas, 12 days before they were due to be released, and the Amarillo post office sold out of its share of the stamps in December 1992, making it an unofficial 'first day issue'.

## Elvis lives on in Hollywood

The popularity of the entertainer who has been dead for more than two decades continues to grow, and years after his death the Elvis remains a cultural icon, recognizable all over the world. Elvis's material continues to be used in new works. In the feature movie *Lethal Weapon* released in 1987, Elvis's 1957 recording 'I'll be home for Christmas' is heard over the closing credits. Tuesday Weld, who starred with Elvis in *Wild in the Country* and who was once linked romantically with the singer, stars in the movie *Heartbreak Hotel*, which was produced by Touchstone Pictures. The film, which got its name from Elvis's first hit single, has Weld running the Flaming Star Hotel. The hotel's name is taken from Elvis's 1960 movie *Flaming Star*. In the movie *Heartbreak Hotel* Tuesday Weld is beaten up by her boyfriend. Her son, determined to help his mother, plots to kidnap Elvis and bring him to his mother's hotel.

**63**

Hollywood still isn't finished with Elvis. In 1992 the movie *Honeymoon in Vegas* culminates with a scene in which the star, Nicholas Cage, parachutes into Las Vegas with a troop of sky-divers called the 'Flying Elvis'; they have black, combed-back hair, white, rhinestone-studded jump-suits and gaudy jewellery. This movie featured 13 Elvis impersonators and many Elvis hits.

## Elvis in politics

In 1992 Elvis made an appearance on the Presidential campaign trail; both political conventions sported buttons proclaiming 'I saw Elvis at the Democratic National Convention' in New York City and 'I saw Elvis at the Republican National Convention' in Houston, Texas.

Presidents Bush and Clinton are not the only ones to have tried to capture their moment with Elvis. In January 1993 the Richard Nixon Presidential Library in Yorba Linda, California, issued Nixon/Elvis White House wristwatches for $45. The library also offered a large postcard featuring Elvis and Nixon on the occasion of the singer's visit to the Oval Office in 1970.

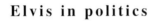

## Fame and clebrity

On what would have been Elvis's 60th birthday, *Life* magazine featured a photograph of him on the cover. Elvis's name was not shown, and even though it was a decade and a half since his death, there was no need to name him – everyone in American recognized him.

Elvis lives on in other ways. In 1991 Lewis Grizzard noted that CNN had reported that 50 per cent of Americans believed that Elvis was still alive. In 1992 CNS news magazine *48 Hours* revealed that 44 per cent of Americans were Elvis fans. The Graceland publicity kit boasts that there are more than 450 Elvis fan clubs in the world, more than for any other celebrity.

Even now, Elvis has the largest number of compact discs available of any recording artist; his songs continue to be heard and the legend lives on.